Oh Fiddlesticks!

By Tanji Dewberry

Illustrated by Suzanne DeSimone

To my angel face, I love you all the time, I love you 'cause you're mine, I love you everyday, I love you so I'll say...

Dewberry, your spirit carried me through...

© 2012 Copyright pending
Self Published by Tanji Dewberry
Design and Illustrations by Suzanne DeSimone
Illustration photography by Brent Van Wieringen
ISBN 978-0-9882708-0-0

Oh Fiddlesticks!

By Tanji Dewberry

Illustrated by Suzanne DeSimone

I love going to the park, and I was taking my favorite truck. My truck is the best. It is yellow, with big wheels and a huge back to hold blocks.

"Ok crew, it's time to go to work. We are going to build the tallest tower in the world."

This means WAR, Chris. War, I say.

You're no longer my friend.

We cannot play."

Chris just laughed and ran away.

When I get upset, I'm not sure what to do.

I got so angry. I kicked the dirt! I stubbed my toe. Boy, did it hurt!

I was so mad. I began to feel crummy. I felt sick on the inside, especially my tummy.

The anger kept building. I started to shake. I felt like I was having an enormous

EARTHQUAKE!!!

My face turned red. I covered my eyes. I stood alone. I started to cry.

Ahhhhhhhhhh!!!

Oh fiddlesticks!

"Sam, you weren't nice to Chris," said Mommy. "He only wanted to play.

Do you want to talk about why you acted that way?"

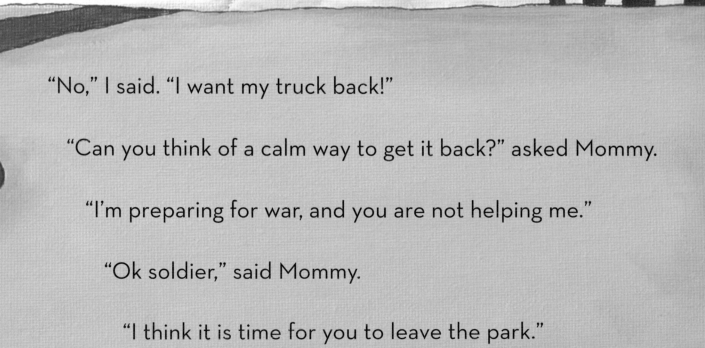

"No," I said. "I want my truck back!"

"Can you think of a calm way to get it back?" asked Mommy.

"I'm preparing for war, and you are not helping me."

"Ok soldier," said Mommy.

"I think it is time for you to leave the park."

When I got home, it was time to eat.
I was still so mad I was fuming in my seat.
I hate peas and carrots. I reached down
and gave them to my dog, Albert.

"Eat your peas and carrots, Sam!"
said Mommy.

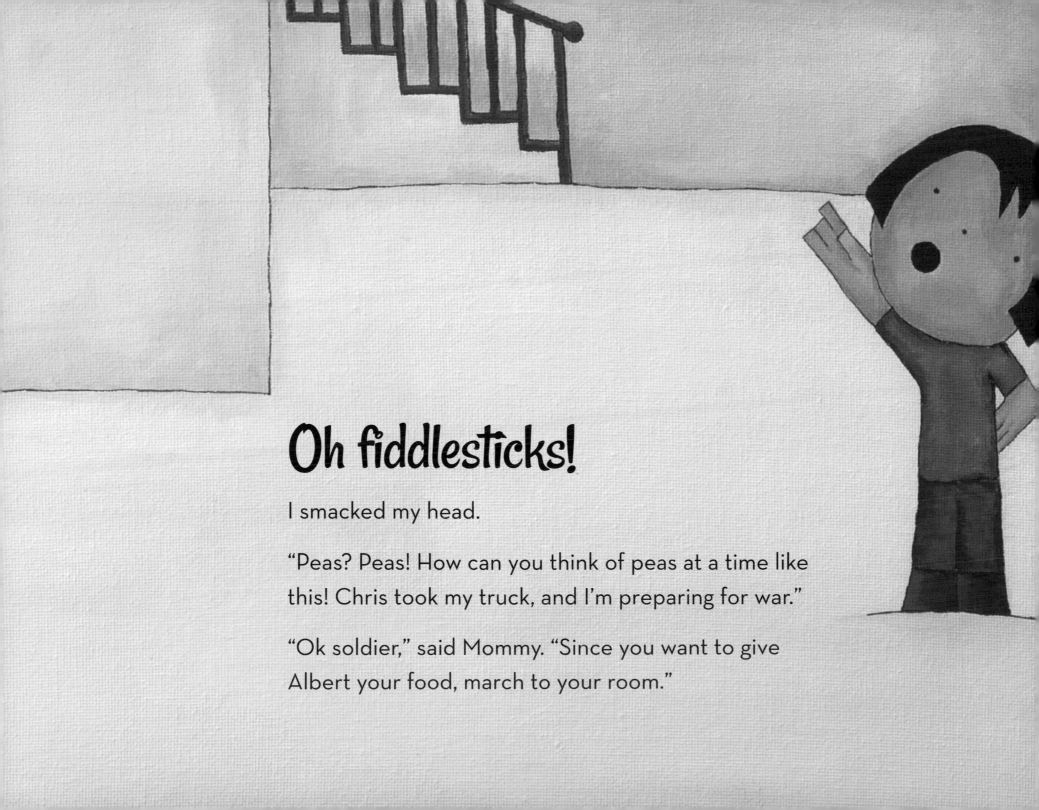

Oh fiddlesticks!

I smacked my head.

"Peas? Peas! How can you think of peas at a time like this! Chris took my truck, and I'm preparing for war."

"Ok soldier," said Mommy. "Since you want to give Albert your food, march to your room."

Boom! Boom! Boom! Up the stairs, I went. I tried to calm down with all of my might.
The anger kept building with no end in sight.
All I wanted was my truck back!

Crash! Crash! Crash!
I made a mess. I didn't care,
I must confess.

"Sam, what have you done to your room?" said Dad. "I know you are angry, but you clean up right now!"

Oh fiddlesticks!

"I want my truck, Dad.
I'm really mad."

"How will you get your truck back?" asked Dad.

Ah hah! I said.

"I'll dress up as a warrior lord with my sword and cape.

Chris will be no match for me.
He will pay the price, just wait and see."

"Maybe you should give more thought to your plan."

"Humpf!" I said. "You are not helping me either."

All through the night I tossed and turned. Finally, morning came
and I rushed to get dressed:
shirt, pants, cape, and sword...

Hmm, I was missing something. Oh forget it. I didn't have time to waste.
All I could think about was my truck.
I was ready to gooooooo!!!
When I got to the playground I looked all around. Then all of a sudden...

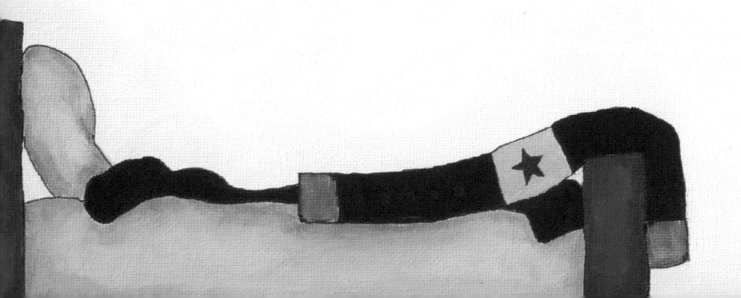

There was Chris and all of my friends. They laughed. I glared.
"Enough laughing! I mean business. Chris, that truck is not yours.
Hand it back now or face my sword!"

"I am not afraid of a warrior with a plastic sword and no pants. Hahaha!"

"I'll be back, Chris!"

1...2...3...4...5...6...

7...8...9...10

"Ugghhhhhhhhhhhh!"

My plan wasn't working. I ran to hide. I had to take care of these

angry feelings inside. A safe space, that's it! I found a tree fast and quick.

I counted to ten.

Oh fiddlesticks!

I still had the anger bug. I gave myself a bear squeeze hug.

I took a deep, deep breath and thought of a new plan.

I needed to fix my pants and relax.

"Maybe if I talk to Chris, I can get my truck back..."

"Chris, the truck is mine.

I need it to build a big, tall building with my crew.

Please give it to me."

"I am a good worker.

Can I help?" said Chris.

"I have a crew already...

buuuut

...SURE! Let's make the tower together!"

Then before I knew it, Chris handed me the truck.

"I just wanted to play with you," he said.

"All you had to do was ask nicely—and bring your belt."

We laughed until our stomachs hurt.

I felt better.

I was okay.

I played with my friend for the rest of the day.

Thank you for reading "Oh Fiddlesticks!".

I hope you enjoyed reading the book as much as I enjoyed writing it.

Emotions are something we all have, but they are the least discussed. Over the last year, I have been working with my son on how to express his emotions in a healthy way, in particular his anger. I am proud to say, he has made tremendous progress! My journey with him was the inspiration for "Oh Fiddlesticks!".

On the right are a few questions to engage young children on anger and how to manage situations when they get upset.

1. In "Oh Fiddlesticks!", Sam gets really mad when Chris takes his truck. Can you think of a time when you were really upset? Can you describe how you felt?

2. Instead of calling Chris names, is there another way Sam could have handled the situation?

3. Can you talk about a time you were upset with a friend? How did you resolve it?

4. Sam has a really hard time talking to his Mom and Dad about his anger. Is there someone you talk to when you are upset?

5. In the end of the book, Sam decides to find a "safe space" where he can calm down. Do you have a "safe space" you go to when you are upset? If not, can you think of an area you can make your "safe space"?

6. What are some of the things Sam does in his "safe space" to calm down?

7. The things Sam does to calm down are called coping skills. There are several coping skills that people can do to help themselves calm down when they are angry. Do you have coping skills that you use? If not, can you think of some?

THANK YOU!

I want to thank all of my family and friends for their love and support over the years and during my writing process. I special thank you to the following: My mother, Cynthia Robinson, my brother, Jajuan Sylvan, Granny Mitchell, the Parkers, La Familia de Hoos, The Dewberry Family, The Mitchell Family, Lamarr Jones, Tim and Joi Russell, Dr. Marilyn Griffin, Charo Figueora, Daree Lewis, Holly Jackson, Joy Collins, Rich Daniels, Garrett Winn, Michelle Paretti, Brenda Belladonna, Rodney Miller, Vern Perry, Ivan Thornton, The Adewoles, Robert Garthe, Esperanza Vargas, T. Michael Johnson, Nadia Anthony, Natalie Oelkers, Emma Vicenzi, Alexandra Koltun, Janice Brown, and Hashim Bello.

A special thank you to my amazing team who helped make my dream a reality: my editor Marlo Garnsworthy, my amazingly talented illustrator Suzanne DeSimone, and my PR gurus at Carte Blanche: Micaeh Johnson and Nyle Washington.